DRI

Martina Evans is an Irish poet and novelist. She grew up in County Cork and is the author of thirteen books of prose and poetry. *American Mules* (2021) won the Pigott Poetry Prize and *The Coming Thing* (2023) was shortlisted for the Derek Walcott Poetry Prize and PEN/Heaney Prize. She is a fellow of the Royal Society of Literature and reviews poetry for the *Irish Times*.

Also by Martina Evans from Carcanet

The Coming Thing
American Mules
Now We Can Talk Openly About Men
The Windows of Graceland
Burnfort, Las Vegas
Petrol
Facing the Public
Can Dentists Be Trusted?
All Alcoholics Are Charmers

MARTINA EVANS

DRUNKEN DRIVING

CARCANET POETRY

First published in Great Britain in 2026 by
Carcanet
Main Library, The University of Manchester
Oxford Road, Manchester, M13 9PP
www.carcanet.co.uk

A CIP catalogue record for this book is
available from the British Library.

ISBN 978 1 80017 563 1

Book design by Andrew Latimer, Carcanet
Typesetting by LiteBook Prepress Services
Printed in Great Britain by SRP Ltd, Exeter, Devon

FSC www.fsc.org MIX Paper | Supporting responsible forestry FSC® C014540

The publisher acknowledges financial
assistance from Arts Council England.

Supported using public funding by ARTS COUNCIL ENGLAND

For Líadáin &
In Memory of Dora

'look out, look out, look out!'

Linton Kwesi Johnson

'When I found that I was a prisoner a sort of wild feeling came over me. I rushed up and down the stairs, trying every door and peering out of every window I could find, but after a little the conviction of my helplessness overpowered all other feelings. When I look back after a few hours I think I must have been mad for the time, for I behaved much as a rat does in a trap.'

Bram Stoker, *Dracula*

DRUNKEN DRIVING

1.

'Come,' he said at last, 'tell me of London…'

DIRTY-GREY, clanging Pentonville Prison gulped me every Wednesday morning & spat me out in four hours, stinking of fixer & developer – my black suede shoes sodden – stiff neck tingling, hand on the gearstick, glued inside Red Astra on the spider-web crossroads at York Way. Why should turning right be a matter of force? I hadn't asked for war. *Clutch!* I said. *Clutch!* Carl, shaking & angry at the mercy of me Behind the Wheel. Would I die on the road because of a drunken driver. Was I as bad as a drunken driver? *But you're doing a great job,* said Carl afterwards. *That's not what you said on the West Way,* I said. *I'm terrified. I want to leave the prison. We can't afford it,* he said. Same for driving lessons, D.I.V.O.R.C.E. & the internet. Then overnight he asked me to step up – right on to the accelerator.

TO HELP AN INMATE TO ESCAPE OR ATTEMPT TO ESCAPE THE MAXIMUM PENALTY IS FIVE YEARS IMPRISONMENT.

2.

... we appeared to fly along...

IT worked out at £135 a month. Doctor Grey showed me round two X-ray departments – HMP Holloway & HMP Pentonville just in case I could do both. It was my lunch hour at the Whittington & when I got into his charcoal Volvo, I left the London I knew. One minute we floated past the Nag's Head – turning right was just nothing to him, he had the special powers – then we were clicking the car doors shut outside Holloway Prison as if we'd been beamed in like two vampires. Some people just knew they were in control of The Wheel. I couldn't believe the smooth glide down Holloway & up Camden Road. He didn't shake with the steel fear of going as fast as thirty miles an hour, his neck in flames, the cloth stuck to his back. In the prison car park he took out a black belt with a chain & a whistle, *You won't be needing one of these, Mrs McGlinchey,* he said.

THERE HAS BEEN A DEMAND FOR SOME TIME FOR A BOOKLET TELLING IN SIMPLE LANGUAGE 'THE RULES OF THE ROAD'.

3.

With strained ears, I listened, and heard downstairs the grinding of the key in the great lock and the falling back of the heavy door.

THE front entrance was glass & when the automatic doors closed, fear wrapped me like black plastic. They gave him keys to put on the chain. There'd been a fight over one of the officer's girlfriends, someone had a black eye. He thought it was funny. I thought it was exciting. If only I was a Lesbian. It would explain everything & Carl would have to let me go. Argued, guilt-ridden & mesmerised out of my own mind – if only I had a doctor's certificate. *This woman is a Certified Lesbian.* Otherwise it would have to be a fatal accident on the road. *Divorce is out while Negative Equity lasts* – Carl was an estate agent. I'd spent so many nights, stiff with worry he'd be killed as I walked round immobilised blood & alcohol-smelling bodies on the X-ray table, I just *turned.* If someone had to have the blood drained out of them, why should it be me? Who took care of Baby.

KNOW THE METHOD OF THE ISSUE, USE OF AND RETURN OF SECURITY KEYS.

4.

Monster, give me my child!

CARL earned four times what I earned in the NHS. *That man saved you from the gutter,* Justin said. *Do you ever stop to thank him?* The corridors were buttery-cream, windowless. How did Dr Grey know his way? I imagined dropping crumbs or a ball of scarlet yarn as he unlocked gate after gate & every time he took out the keys threaded through the pocket of his white coat. Rattling & clanking, we got to a gate where a crowd of girls in grey & white tracksuits holding babies, asked to be let through. *I'm afraid I can't take responsibility for you ladies!* Oh God, why did he say *ladies!* It was bad enough leaving them there. I was ashamed to be beside him. I said if we took a photo the world would rise up against the injustice. *Sadly it wouldn't, Mrs McGlinchy. & you're not allowed to photograph guests of Her Majesty. & what would Linton Kwesi Johnson say*? I asked. *Who is he?* said Dr Grey.

BE AWARE OF THE PROBLEMS INVOLVED IN THE USE OF SECURITY KEYS.

5.

What sort of place had I come to, and among what kind of people?

WOULDN'T *you think the Queen would be pure embarrassed to have her guests treated like this? Oh You Irish!* said Dr Grey. Matron joked him about *the pool. Allow me to introduce Sister Singh!* HMPS was very correct. I must always refer to myself as Mrs McGlinchy, never Imelda, he said. His long legs scissored under his white coat, speeding me through corridors to the dark room – no automatic processer, only wet developing! *I'm grey from writing letters, requesting updated equipment but the wheels are slow in HMPS.* Slow? I'd never even seen a manual dark room in my life, *Maybe you should write to the Queen?* Then we were where he wanted to bring me. The huge room, lit-up, quiet. Royal blue pool, HM's lion shimmering in gold on its floor. *I swim here every Wednesday.* I looked at him, *Yes, I know. It's a shame! What a waste! Never used!* His silver fillings caught the light.

A THICK WHITE LINE ACROSS THE ROAD SHOWS THE POINT AT WHICH THE VEHICLE MUST STOP.

6.

... for certainly if I had been fully awake I must have noticed the approach of such a remarkable place.

THE portal to Pentonville was not new. The main gate looked Victorian, big wooden door, thin slat of glass to look out. An officer let us in & Dr Grey collected his keys, joking about his lovely assistant & nothing about watching out for the *Pentonville* prison officers. Only Lesbians were wolves. The Holloway visit had been cream corridors & a stinking darkroom but this was walking right through the lion's den because the hospital was in the middle of the prison, a metal cage with greying canvas hung across the landings to stop the prisoners from throwing themselves off. I could see the prisoners' cells with their thick sallow doors. I didn't notice the smell or the dirt at first. The X-ray room seemed okay. Another Deane Mobile, a newer unit, a Phillips but the dark room – shit! My neck creaked. Wet developing again.

PAY PARTICULAR ATTENTION TO THE OUTSIDE WALL.
LOOK FOR CRACKS, FRESH PAINT AND TAP WALLS
FOR HOLLOW SOUNDS.

7.

I read that every known superstition in the world is gathered into the horseshoe of the Carpathians...

MANUAL developing was spoken about by silver-haired radiographers who had mortgages of £9 a month because they'd been around so long & two-inch wobbling ash piles on the end of their Silk Cuts. Moll Finn, who smoked Major & was the only one able for the roaring surgeons of Cork Regional, told stories of radiographers' slippery fingers dropping undeveloped gall bladders in the theatre or the radiographer who was also a ballerina opening the dark room hatch to see a surgeon's Dracula face screaming on the other side. *One fecking fogged film!* said Molly from her funnel of smoke. Wet developing was like drawing water from a well. Or oil lamps & horse-drawn carriages & I'd seen one of them already that morning, a glass hearse with black horses & red & white faced mourners, sooty plumes nodding on the horses' heads as they trotted down Holloway Road.

TRAFFIC SIGNS, TRAFFIC LIGHTS AND THE DUTY TO KNOW AND USE HAND SIGNALS APPLY FULLY TO A PERSON DRIVING A HORSE AND CART.

8.

I would watch my colonial tongue if I were you.

I GOT a card with a chain that said VISITOR, sat in a cold draughty room, dirty hard wooden benches. Staircase in the corner. The man on the gate rang over for someone to get me. A man came in a black & white check sports coat, grey briefcase under his arm – Dan, a teacher *of Mechanical Drawing,* from Cavan or maybe Monaghan. Or was it West Meath? It might have been Roscommon. All those counties meant nothing to me – only a memory of the blank map in National School & the Master's roaring whiskey breath, *Point out the town of Athlone!* I rarely met anyone from Cork. *Do you know Oscar Wilde spent time here?* I bowed with an imperceptible nod & *Roger Casement was hanged in the yard.* I did know but I was Undercover & didn't want anyone to know what I was thinking. What was Dan thinking? The officer in the corner had his head down. I looked up the filthy stairs.

THE SECURITY OFFICE IS SITUATED ABOVE AND TO THE RIGHT OF THE MAIN GATE. AS YOU WOULD EXPECT ALL ASPECTS OF SECURITY ARE DEALT WITH BY THIS DEPARTMENT. THE COLLATING OF ALL INFORMATION HOWEVER TRIVIAL IS PIECED TOGETHER WITH OTHER INFORMATION TO CREATE A BETTER PICTURE OF WHAT IS HAPPENING.

9.

Enter freely and of your own will!

DAN was halfway through reciting *The Ballad of Reading Gaol* in the sing-song voice of a child from National School when boots tapped on the stairs & a white-faced officer, Phil, shouted, *Who's for collection?* Desperate banging clanged like there was scaffolding going up as we went through. Where was the centre of the Panopticon Eye? *Invented by a Utilitarian*, reminding me of Dora & Justin's tarry-black disgusted eye. *Don't remind me of Utilitarianism please*! Dora said when I rang from Dr Foot's secret international line at the Whittington. In the middle of the cage, a giant blonde officer stopped us – Mr Barnsley, the dark room technician. When Dr Grey said Mr Barnsley would show me the ropes, I said, *Pentonville – the Home of Ropes!* & Dr Grey said not to make that joke with Mr Barnsley who'd been taking the X-rays because they couldn't get a radiographer. I should've seen that red flag from the start.

YOUR ID CARD IS THE AUTHORISATION TO ENTER THE PRISON AND SHOULD BE CARRIED ON YOUR PERSON AT ALL TIMES.

10.

Suddenly, away on our left, I saw a faint flickering blue flame. The driver saw it at the same moment; he at once checked the horses, and, jumping to the ground, disappeared into the darkness.

MR Barnsley'd been taking the X-rays & according to Dr Grey was the *best radiographer* he'd ever met. I coughed loudly & redly. Dr Grey said, *Do you need water, Mrs McGlinchey? Well, you're worrying me,* I said, *because I can't do wet developing. Oh no need to be jealous, I prefer you,* said Dr Grey. & so I had to follow in the black polished footsteps of the best radiographer ever who didn't even need to train. *He'll be thrilled to assist,* said Dr Grey, his head black against the white light box, talking into his dictaphone… *Myocardial Infarct… ahem.* It was like he'd inhaled some sulphurous Tough-Guy prison gas. Maybe he was afraid his spirit would be broken by the prison system. Or was he joking because he'd very cold feet about me doing the job too. What if the original offer'd been a joke he couldn't get out of? Were we both trapped?

SHOW AND PHYSICALLY GO THROUGH WITH THE NEW MEMBER OF STAFF THE USE OF CELL AND PASS KEYS AND IN PARTICULAR THE METHOD OF NOT LOCKING ONESELF INTO A CELL.

11.

The only light was the flickering rays of our own lamps…

I COULDN'T swim, was driving by chance & only knew automatic film processing. Mr Barnsley knew everything & could drive lorries. Probably a powerful swimmer when he wasn't overpowering prisoners. He had a pot belly & very long legs that looked like two extra people inside his black trousers. His shoes were black mirrors & he smiled every time I called him Mr Barnsley. I had the feeling he had a feeling Dr Grey'd made a mistake too. But it didn't seem hard that first morning with only a finger & a cervical spine. I told Mr Barnsley that manual processing hadn't been in hospitals for decades & he nodded in an impermeable way as he towered inside in the dark room. Mr Barnsley didn't waste words & was the best radiographer ever without training *which only goes to show*, Dr Grey said.

GET AN EXPERIENCED DRIVER TO EXPLAIN THE CONTROLS TO YOU.

12.

Must you go? Oh! young Herr, must you go?

I'LL *give you one big bit of advice* said Mr Barnsley as we stood in the dark room over stinking vinegary vats of developer & fixer swirling the X-rays & I waited for the key to wet developing to be made known. *Never reveal, whatever you do, never reveal your Christian name to a prisoner.* I sagged in the hammock of darkness. *Pick your side early on,* he said. Did he know I was Undercover? The dim blood-red light veiled my red face as I agreed in a voice of equal granite. Was Mr Barnsley from Yorkshire or was it just his name? England was another grey blank map to me. I put my foot on a box of Kodak like it was the rung of a bar & stuck out my hip, *I so will,* I said, *NOT give my Christian name.* He was quiet. I got a queasy feeling as if we were both floating in a vapour of blood. & then he said, *They'll go for you because you're soft.*

DO NOT DISCUSS ANY PERSONAL INFORMATION WITH INMATES. YOU COULD LEAVE YOURSELF OPEN TO MANIPULATION AND/OR THREATS.

13.

… the crowd round the inn door, which had by this time swelled to a considerable size,all made the sign of the cross and pointed two fingers towards me.

THE first weeks after Mr Barnsley had gone – back to whatever he was doing before I came – were desperate. I missed him. I asked Carl if he thought I had Stockholm syndrome & he said *he wouldn't have said it only I'd said it myself.* Nurses & officers dropped patients in the holding cell & left me alone. I asked them to stay & they said they couldn't although a few did. Furtively. One steely woman said she *appreciated my vulnerable position. But Dr Grey said I'd never be alone! He's an outsider!* she said. The workload doubled, trebled, quadrupled. Christian names were the last thing on my mind. I was just getting them through in time for Dr Grey. They came into the room in any order so I was never ready. I didn't know who was coming & then I was on my own with them & had to leave them on the table while I dripped around the dark room, my face a red ball of stress.

IF FOR ANY REASON YOU ARE UNABLE TO PHYSICALLY ASSIST YOURSELF YOU MUST ENSURE YOU FIND A MEMBER OF STAFF WHO CAN. DO NOT WALK AWAY MUTTERING 'WELL IT'S NOTHING TO DO WITH ME!'

14.

... great frowning rocks guarded us boldly on either side.

OH *that Irish temper, it's so sexy!* said Cyril who was very young & wore one winking red earring. I'd been kicking the Phillips with my sodden black foot to show I wasn't soft. It groaned & shuddered & died as I pressed the greasy white button on & off. Cyril's voice was squashed from the sandbag I put under his head, his knees bent for a lateral lumbar spine, face on his two hands like an angel, staring at me until I was as red as the dark room safelights. Pins & needles passed over me. Out in three weeks & he wanted me to come to his reggae party. He was very intense. *Stay there!* I said. I was sure I'd been firm but when I stood on the sodden newspapers, swirling the films in the vinegar air of the dark room, he touched my shoulder & I screamed. We were so frightened, we ran out together. Or maybe he just couldn't bear the terrible smell.

METHODS OF RAISING AN ALARM

1. *Alarm Bell*
2. *Whistle*
3. *Telephone*
4. *UHP Radio*
5. *Word of Mouth (shouting)*

15.

I descended, minding carefully where I went, for the stairs were dark, being only lit by loopholes in the heavy masonry.

IF *they follow me into the dark room, no one can hear me call!* Dr Cherry's eyes became two currants in his head. *Don't talk to them, stop engaging with them. But I can't ignore them when they're locked up 24/7 & fit to burst. The Irish ones are the worst,* I said to throw him off the scent of Cyril & then an image of Mick Wolf from the Whittington appeared to me roaring *JUDAS!* his wine face darkening under his Mr Whippy combover. *They're lonely. They want to know what county I'm from. What county?* said Dr Cherry. *You know like Limerick or West Meath? I'm from Cork, by the way!* & at that his two currant eyes tightened like there was a screwdriver at the back of his head. *Look!* he roared & I jumped back. *You say, Sit down & Shut up. You're the liar, the thief, the junkie you always were. Sit down, shut up & take your X-ray like a man.*

WHILST AT WORK YOU ARE PART OF A TEAM AND AS SUCH MUST WORK IN HARMONY WITH OTHER STAFF.

16.

I am surely in the toils. Last night the Count asked me in the suavest tones to write three letters.

IF Dr Cherry's eyes were like currants, mine must have dilated like burst black grapes. His sweet voice returned, *I'm sorry, I just don't have the resources. No, leave the door open. I need to keep an eye on things.* The All-important Eye that only saw what it wanted to see. They didn't even have a proper Panopticon! I walked away, looking at my scuffed shoes, not black any more, grey from chemicals. My stained white dress, I needed black trousers & black shoes like Mr Barnsley. I stood out in white. Things were so bad, sometimes I wanted to *be* Mr Barnsley not a ridiculous fly, half-drowned in chemicals, caught in a web. & why did patients never come at the right time? I expected military precision in a prison but it was all uncertainty. I never knew when things were going to happen. It was like waiting for Carl or working in the Archway Wing of the Whittington.

NOTICE TO ALL PATIENTS

IF YOU HAVE ANY QUESTIONS PLEASE RESERVE THEM FOR THE DOCTOR IN CHARGE OF YOUR CASE. YOU SHOULD NOT INTERRUPT OR DISTRACT THE ATTENTION OF THE RADIOGRAPHER AT ANY TIME.

By order of Dr Cherry, 12/07/1994

17.

He lashed the horses unmercifully… and with wild cries of encouragement urged them on.

JUDAS! Mick Wolf's voice rang through my brain, his salmon-pink corduroy figure driving a wheelchair through the grey corridors of Archway Wing like it was a coach & four. Archway was for old people & AIDS patients. & I thought I'd been banished there too when I became a Senior. Mick brought the patients down in crowds when it suited him, royal purple hungover face seething, whizzing frail skeletons so fast in their chairs. Mary Shea told me I must report him – *You've been made Senior to make a difference. Think of the old people! I am!* I said. But she was nowhere when I stood in the superintendent's office, my face pillar-box red, accused of *no respect* for *a faithful NHS worker of thirty years.* & so Mick kept bringing the patients when it suited him, all at once, at speed. He hissed like Granddad. & like Carl, he liked playing tricks in the dark.

DON'T SPEED.

18.

The baying of the wolves sounded nearer and nearer, as though they were closing round on us from every side. I grew dreadfully afraid…

WHAT made the wind rage in Archway, was it the towers or its position between Highgate Hill & Archway Road? When I mentioned the howling to Mick, he smiled through the glow red cigarette bobbing between his purple lips. He brought down Alfred Peck who had no legs & Sister Black came too, carrying a pair of artificial limbs because she thought Mr Peck should stand for his X-ray. I could not imagine where or how the legs would be attached without suffering. *You can still see the fluid levels if he's in the sitting position.* Mick & Sister Black helped me get Mr Peck propped up & I slid the gun-metal grey cassette behind his back. When they were gone & I was alone in the winter-black I thought I could hear Mick's trainers squeaking on the lino. But when I went out there was no one, only a tan leg with a white knee-high sock & a black polished shoe leaning up against the wall.

MISSING ITEMS SHOULD BE REPORTED TO SECURITY AS SOON AS POSSIBLE.

19.

His redeeming quality is a love of animals...

MICK drank my scream like it was a fresh pint of Guinness. Sister Black hadn't noticed him hanging on to one leg when they left. *And you were only worried about Mr Peck!* I told him it was the worst fright I ever got & now I was helping him to feed the mauve & grey pigeons, flinging lumps of sliced pan out the staffroom window. I asked if he ever hit anyone with a lump & he said no one would know where the bread was raining from. We smoked my Silk Cut or his Players. He spoke about overtime in the morgue, *The fridge was FULL!* & I had to guess his age which was a Fierce Complicated subtraction under pressure because the drink made him look much older & I admired his salmon corduroy flares – *only 10p!* from the Academic Centre jumble sale & when he mentioned Rachel Hatred, I could hardly believe such an unusual surname.

COMMUNICATION IS OF CENTRAL IMPORTANCE IN EVERY FUNCTION. IT IS VERY IMPORTANT THAT MESSAGES, INFORMATION AND IDEAS ARE PASSED AND RECEIVED APPROPRIATELY AND EFFECTIVELY.

20.

I never liked garlic before, but to-night it is delightful!

YOU *could die* said Dora. But *YOU have signed the Official Secrets Act as part of your training* said the big pile of stapled pages I was given after my security talk. I sat in the flat, waiting for Carl's unsteady footstep on the stairs, his white face, orange hair flaming against the dark suit. I didn't want to think of my heart muscle bulging red-hot & wet, all that liquid inside my skin, touching the white cotton of my uniform. I was going grey with the fear. Only 33 years of age & Carl found one grey hair on my head at the weekend. Would he be sober enough to be a comfort or just desperate, spouting Pádraig Pearse, *the beauty of this world hath made me sad… This beauty that will pass,* he kept saying that after he found the grey hair. His pupils huge & black in his white face, fork toying with the rusty goulash made so many hours before. *Maybe a bit too much paprika?* he said.

ASK NEW STAFF IF THEY UNDERSTAND THE 1952 PRISONS ACT PARAGRAPHS SECTIONS 39, 40, AND 41 (SECTIONS ABOVE).

21.

He knows that I know too much…

MY heart melted & boiled, forcing its red liquid aspect into my mind. Was it getting ready to blow like the men on the roof of Strangeways Prison? Those prisoners got the keys to the fridge with the good steaks & fried them up rebelliously. *Lose your keys!* the security training man said. *Every single lock in the prison will have to be changed. Would you like that*? Myself & the other woman said we would not like that. *Now don't be telling prisoners your personal details. No way!* said the other woman, looking at me as if I was going to. *They creep into your confidence, all over you like a rash and when they have enough ammunition, they strike!* His knee clanged the black rung of the chair. *Women can't stop falling in love with prisoners. Lonely vulnerable women, usually teachers.* Was he looking at me? The woman was nodding her head. *I'm not a teacher,* I said.

YOU SHOULD NOT ALLOW YOURSELF TO GET INVOLVED EMOTIONALLY WITH INMATES. SOME CAN BE VERY PERSUASIVE.

22.

My host, who stood on one side of the great fireplace, leaning against the stonework, made a graceful wave of his hand…

AREN'T *you?* He looked down at his notes & me in my white nurse's uniform nearly strangled with my grey nurse's belt & my black Pentonville belt & my keys & my chain & my whistle. The whistle I thought would work until I was called in to see *The Governor*. The Warden smiled as if he was just tickled by someone very small making a very big fuss. *Everyone else has to work single-handed.* He told me my whistle wouldn't work if I just put my lips to it *like that*. I stared at him. *Are you listening? I certainly am!* I said. I'd been relying on the whistle – that's if I could get my hands free as they were forever sunk in murky vats of chemicals. *Like everything else in life it needs practice!* But it wasn't as if I could practise in the prison. *And you can't practise at home either!* He said I'd be *brought up for noise nuisance.*

BE AWARE OF YOUR ROLE IN THE EFFECTIVE MANAGEMENT OF THE SECURITY OF THE ESTABLISHMENT.

23.

At the edge of Hampstead Heath we heard a policeman's heavy tramp.

TAKE *a stroll up to a quiet part of Hampstead Heath at the weekends and practice,* said the Warden. But Carl was writing his novel on Sunday mornings now & always came home late. Worse was the *plámás.* The black cab late in the night, ticking expensively in the cul de sac. The unsteady footsteps. Two dozen shite red roses in plastic & how all the girls in the office were asking for me. The ratchet of the arm of the record player, George & Tammy singing how life can be rough but the faith between them made the love grow. I was Fierce Sick of it but the old mesmerism worked sometimes or I pretended it did because I was also Fierce Tired. *Don't let the prisoners see your keys. They read them with one sweep of the eye & go off & make a copy out of a bar of soap in their spare time & they've plenty of it because they're banged up permanently because of staff shortages.* But how could you make a key out of a bar of soap?

THE MEMBER OF STAFF SHOULD KEEP HIS/HER KEYS OUT OF SIGHT OF PRISONERS WHENEVER POSSIBLE, ESPECIALLY DURING INTERVIEWS AND SITUATIONS WHERE A PRISONER WOULD HAVE A LONG TIME TO STUDY THE KEYS.

24.

There is the sound of hammering; it is the box being nailed down.

DORA didn't want to hear about Jeremy Bentham, *Will I always be reminded of my youthful stupidity?* But I wanted to talk to *someone* about the history of Pentonville. No more hobnobbing like they did in Newgate. Victorian prisoners spun oakum in solitary cells. They weren't allowed one word, couldn't even look at each other – in the exercise yard, they had to wear cloth masks. Separate cubicles in the chapel. *For every sixty thousand persons imprisoned in Pentonville, 220 cases of insanity, 210 cases of delusion & 40 suicides.* I saw signs about not touching the knots on the ropes round prisoners' necks when cutting them down. They were keeping refugees in the prison. Imagine thinking you'd escaped & ending up behind bars! *& where were they getting the ropes?* Dora wanted to know. *Maybe they're making them out of bars of soap, too,* I said or leftover oakum & Dora said this was no time for jokes.

STRESS THAT KEYS NEED NOT ONLY BE COPIED BY IMPRESSIONS ON BARS OF SOAP – SOME PRISONERS CAN 'READ' KEYS QUICKLY BY JUST LOOKING AT THEM. KEYS SHOULD BE SECURED TO A KEY CHAIN PRIOR TO LEAVING THE GATE LODGE.

25.

...do we not see our duty? Yes! And do we not promise to go on to the bitter end?

LINTON Kwesi Johnson called *look out, look out!* from the cassette every time I drove away, a stiff corpse in Red Astra. Everything was ready to blow like the Bastille only the storm was *inside* – an angry ball of hot steam. *Security is an all-round occupation. You should be alert and vigilant at all times.* But what about when you're peering up at a dripping X-ray held against the bleeding-red safelights because you can't see a thing after some fool painted the dark room black? The patient *unattended* on the table? Why didn't they worry about *lonely vulnerable* women ready to fall in love with a prisoner then? The security talk circled back to the keys & it was Fierce Boring with Big Diagrams. Class 1, Class 1 (Cell), Class 2, Class 3. Was I a locksmith now on top of everything else? & then when he gave us a stapled bundle of pages, I realised that I'd read it already. Could you sign the Official Secrets Act twice?

KEY CHAINS SHOULD NOT BE TOO LONG (OTHERWISE THE WHOLE BUNCH WILL CRASH TO THE FLOOR) OR TOO SHORT (OTHERWISE THEY WILL NOT REACH THE LOCK).

26.

I can hear the key withdraw: then another door opens and shuts; I hear the creaking of lock and bolt.

I'D been given that booklet already with my black belt, chain & whistle – which I'd *never* been advised to practise on. They lost my first ID card so I had to go through the photographing twice. The same officers laughing & joking as if it needed five of them to take a photo. I wanted to know how the *Lesbians* photographed *their* fellow staff in Holloway. But Holloway was never mentioned again. Not by me. Not by Dr Grey although he was surprised to see I had a belt now, too. The officer at the front desk said I must sit down & read *the whole thirty pages* in front of him. But I said I had to pick up Baby from nursery so he let me take it home because (he said) he was *A big softy. Read it carefully without a word to no one because it should never leave these prison walls,* his last seven words rang like a slide guitar.

WHEN GIVEN AN IDENTITY CARD YOU WILL BE EXPECTED TO READ AND UNDERSTAND THE REVERSE SIDE.

27.

...feel the hot breath on my neck...

THE summer was very heavy. Thunder rumbled as I crossed the yard expecting a break-out. Imagining prisoners on the roof even though I'd never even seen the roof. My eyes on my stained feet as I walked through, locking & unlocking gates, red-faced. The dark room baked & the greasy tape fixing the window-blind to the wall melted, letting ashy fingers of light into the dark room. I held my back to the vent to shield the films from getting fogged. Hard enough getting X-rays for them to be ruined & I shrieked quietly like a vampire afraid of incendiary light. My neck lit with pain, I made desperate mistakes, left a box of Kodak open with the light on, got artifacts & smudges on the films. The chemicals weren't evenly distributed because there wasn't time to agitate the developer. Drip marks ran down the dried films like a bad paint job & Dr Grey kept saying, *Excellent! Excellent, Mrs McGlinchy!*

IF DAZZLED, SLOW DOWN AND STOP.

28.

Then there came the sound of many feet tramping and dying away in some passage which sent up a clanging echo.

WHEN I worried about X-ray quality, Mr. Barnsley looked at me, *They're prisoners. They're going Nowhere.* When I repeated a pelvis because there was an artefact over the iliac crest & worried about radiation, he said the same, *He's going Nowhere.* A prisoner stood with his black hood up like a mediaeval personification of death, reading Dr Cherry's notice aloud outside the X-ray door. *Do not speak to the radiographer, eh?* I was pure scarlet, fitting the key in the lock. Who left him there? *I've a right to know your name!* he said. I'd laughed at Mr Barnsley telling me not to give out my Christian name but I didn't want to be taking orders either. He looked as disgusted as Justin. My eyes were level with his grey elasticated waist. *Do I really have to give you my name?* It hurt my neck to look up at him. *Do I really have to give you my name?* he imitated me in a squeaky cod Irish accent. *It's about respect!*

NEVER LET INMATES UNATTENDED, THEY TEND TO GET LOST.

29.

No piteous cry or agonised entreaty would make them look at me…

SURE *if the rest of the staff have to work on their own. Why can't you?* said Justin on the black phone. He'd been talking to Agnes & Carl. I knew I shouldn't have weakened in front of Agnes. *Do you cause trouble wherever you go? But I'm scared,* I said. *Sure you were born scared &* I wanted to say how scared he'd been of the red-eyed rat in the cat shed. *You're leaning on Agnes, ringing her all the time, moaning. But I only rang her twice, she said she liked the funny stories. It's only £135 a month after tax & the payments are always delayed so I'm talking to the union. Jesus!* said Justin. *You brought the unions in, you Big Commie. No wonder you're scared. Look at Carl's Big Job & what've you brought to him, apart from your student loan? Grey hairs, I'd say. If it's half Irish. they won't touch* you! & the rest? *Yerra, don't mind the blacks,* he said. *They're probably more scared of* you!

YOU SHOULD NOT ALLOW ANY INMATE IN YOUR PARTY TO WALK BEHIND YOU.

30.

… as a child she used to walk in her sleep…

THE Irish prisoners rattled the grey bars mournfully like fellows bound for Van Diemen's Land. Nearly everyone was Irish, West Indian or Nigerian. *Conclusions should be drawn,* agreed Dora. But I had no time for conclusions between Baby, Pentonville, Whittington, cleaning, shopping, cooking, washing & dreading the drive to Fortune Green Road for the MOT. I didn't even have time for lunch & wasn't I after signing the Official Secrets Act? Maybe twice & maybe I'd knocked down a child in a hit & run? I saw the black & white accusing sign nailed to a plane tree when I slowly bumped over the cobbles into our cul de sac, white dress stuck to my back. *Maybe I'd heard a noise like a stone against Red Astra's wheel?* I thought Carl would say it was nothing but he didn't. He said Julian next door had mentioned cowards & that I was to say nothing. My red heart raced faster.

SHOULD YOU BE INVOLVED IN AN INCIDENT WHICH COULD HAVE REPERCUSSIONS IN YOUR WORK YOU SHOULD REPORT IT. THIS APPLIES ESPECIALLY IF YOU HAVE TO APPEAR IN COURT CHARGED WITH A CRIMINAL OFFENCE, OR TO ANSWER A CIVIL ACTION, SPEEDING FINES SHOULD BE REPORTED.

31.

... doors, doors, doors everywhere, and all locked and bolted.

THE phone rang & sure it was Dora, I lifted it on the second ring. But as soon as I put the black receiver to my ear, I heard the intake of a *Hamlet*, saw the red-hot glow on the tip of his donkey-grey cigar, his lemon fingers flicking it, *You'd want to be very careful with the Prevention Of Terrorism Act. Quieter Irish people than you have been banged up for years for less blackguarding. Is there nowhere where you won't be acting the notice box? Have you no fear? I'm terrified,* I said. *They're shouting at me from the minute I go through the gates. Yerra go way outta that you're loving it.* I couldn't tell him that Carl lost his licence. That was another Official Secrets Act. I couldn't ever mention Tower Bridge where he was arrested or Carl would say I was jeering at him. Even when other people mentioned Tower Bridge, I went vermillion. *I don't know how that man puts up with you,* said Justin. *He must have the patience of Job.*

IN FOGGY WEATHER BE EXTRA CAREFUL.

32.

We found the child awake... Dr Vincent took the bandage from its throat, and showed us the punctures.

SUNDAY evening Carl said I *couldn't* have killed the child because I was going five miles an hour with the window open & there were witnesses when I parked Red Astra. *And the child's only injured. I wish you said that in the first place!* But the doubt was set like concrete now. When I said Pentonville was a Chamber of Horrors, Justin said, *You've got an imagination. I'll give you that. But I don't need one!* I said. *Half of Madame Tussaud's waxworks were hanged there.* Justin snorted, *Highly-strung like yourself?* I could almost see his grey smoke blowing through the holes in the black receiver. I said it had been a training school for hangmen & Justin said *Jesus, will you put on Carl there, my head is ringing. Do you agree that every man kills the thing he loves?* I said to Dora afterwards & she said, *Fuck Oscar Wilde!* & I said *Yes, Fuck Oscar Wilde!* I'd just read his favourite novel *Melmoth the Wanderer* & it was Fierce Boring.

BEFORE YOU MOVE OFF MAKE SURE IT IS SAFE TO DO SO.

33.

...it seemed to me as though something dark stood behind the seat where the white figure shone...

CHICKENPOX had polka-dotted Baby red & white all over & I was lying beside her in the dark, reciting poems, singing songs to stop the scratching when the phone rang. I went to the cold black receiver – had Justin thought of another desperate thing to say? I thought I heard singing on the line. George Jones moaning it was four in the morning, *With the blood from my body I could start my own still... if drinking don't kill me...* & then I heard Carl, *I'll be late, near ten.* But Carl never rang & I didn't want to say that ten was early for him because he'd nearly caught fire that morning when I said it was only thirty minutes from London Bridge to Drayton Park not *two fucking hours* & one glass of red wine didn't smell like ten pints. Back in bed, Baby was red-hot, the covers were off & I was singing *Down by the Salley Gardens* when the front door banged.

TAKE SPECIAL CARE AT TWILIGHT.

34.

There was undoubtedly something, long and black,
bending over the half-reclining figure.

AT FIRST, I thought it was the man in flat below but as the footsteps began to climb our stairs, Baby's hot soft bare legs kicked out. I wanted to cover her but couldn't move myself. The footsteps kept coming, so sure of themselves & then the flat door opened as if the lock was pure butter. I pulled the duvet over Baby but she kicked it off again. I turned off the pink lamp. The footsteps went into the kitchen. The kettle switched on & then the TV. The confidence! & I had nothing to fight with only beanie babies. Baby was quiet. Maybe he would go away. I tried again to cover Baby, lying so red & white & raw. The footsteps climbed again, the bathroom door opened, taps ran & finally when our door slowly opened, the black shape was Carl. *Surprise!* He laughed all night, the memory of my terrified face *a pure scream.*

SHOULD YOU SEE OR HEAR ANYTHING OUT OF THE ORDINARY, YOU SHOULD SUBMIT AN SIR (SECURITY INFORMATION REPORT) TO THE SECURITY DEPARTMENT.

35.

But these things are no proof, for they may have been evidences that my mind was not as usual...

RED Astra glided away with me like a hearse & I wasn't sure I could feel the pedals. While I was adjusting the mirror, a black & white street sign flashed– *Hilldrop Crescent!* – where Dr Crippen murdered his wife with Hyoscin. I'd turned right instead of left on Camden Road. Was I to be trusted at all? Was I possessed? Maybe I *was* the perpetrator in a hit & run too? I wished I could ask Mr Barnsley about ghosts in the prison. When I asked him if bullying went on, he said, *None at all!* But half the X-rays were for assault, usually by the police. Or other prisoners. One prisoner took his iron bed apart & beat another prisoner into a pinky-red pulp with it. Or so they said. I hadn't come across a prison officer assault but they were hardly going to write that down. I had a few elbows where arms were twisted behind prisoner's backs but that left no bruising or fractures.

ALWAYS CONSULT YOUR MIRROR BEFORE YOU MOVE OFF.

36.

There were a few feathers about the room and on his pillow a drop of blood.

I DIDN'T want to think of Mr Barnsley, my only friend in the prison, twisting arms & telling prisoners they were *going nowhere.* The prisoners might think I was on his side since that second week when Dr Jigg requested a PA & Lateral chest on a raging redhead. I ignored the request for a lateral like we did on the outside but Jigg must have been a big shot because Dr Grey frowned, *Where's the lateral? But he didn't need it! No. You have to do what they ask for in here. We have to have a lateral.* I whitened. *But the patient is gone back!* Getting a prisoner down even once was a feat. Mr Barnsley butted in, *The patient refused to have an X-ray! Oh, is that right?* said Dr Grey. *That's right I just witnessed it,* said Mr Barnsley & Dr Grey wrote it down on the notes. *Mr Barnsley's got your back,* he said, swinging out past us in his dazzling white coat.

IT SHOULD CONTAIN AS MUCH INFORMATION AS POSSIBLE, NAMES, PLACES, ACTS, THREATS, ETC.

37.

Hark! in the courtyard and down the rocky way the roll of heavy wheels, the crack of whips, and the chorus of the Szgany as they pass into the distance.

AFTER I'd escaped Hilldrop Crescent, I was late to Roman Way. I went to the corner shop to get Wrigley's Spearmint because my mouth got so dry in the dark room. An old woman stood beside me at the counter with two blue toilet rolls. Trying to remember what else she came for. All ahead of me, I thought with my one grey hair. At the gates, a white lorry was driving out so I didn't need to ring the bell. There were cheerful officers on the gate for once. I could see the Galway officer with the pale cavernous face waving a black Securicor van through the inner gates with her left hand, cup & red-tipped fag in her right, her huge spare frame buried inside a black overcoat, ash-blonde hair high above the pale dome of her forehead like Tammy Wynette. She always asked about Baby & she asked me again today. I told her about the chickenpox & she clucked sympathetically, smiling, looking like a ghost herself.

ALL COMMUNICATIONS VIA UHF RADIO ARE PASSED THROUGH THE CONTROLLER ON SECURITY.

38.

'You may go anywhere you wish in the castle, except where the doors are locked, where of course you will not wish to go.'

I NOTICED another round mirror over the outer gate. Were there prisoners in the van? *Six is it you've got?* asked the officer doing the register. I looked jealously at the driver's pale hands on the steering wheel. Another one in Control of the Wheel. My keys rattled out of the chute & I went inside the barbed wire. The big yard was lonely. I supposed the wife-killers from the Chamber of Horrors exercised there. They might be glad to have the black hoods over their faces. A can tumbled on the concrete. Grey clouds smoked overhead & I wished I understood the layout instead of running blindly through like a rat every Wednesday. Plastic sheeting & some machinery reminded me of a farmyard. Hard to believe I was still in London. I thought of farm boys in prison although it was mostly Dubs I X-rayed despite all the shouting of *Monaghan! Leitrim! Roscommon!* through the bars.

WHILE ESCORTING INMATES FROM ONE AREA TO ANOTHER YOU MUST BE AWARE OF THE NUMBER OF INMATES IN YOUR CARE.

39.

She doesn't know her mind a bit; she seems to see the storm coming, but can't decide…

I WAS bent over the table in the office leafing through X-ray forms, groaning quietly to myself. *What the hell!* I said. How long more could I take the roaring & shouting & whistling & *County Roscommon! & have you ever been to Ballybunion? Help me, God,* I groaned as the door swung back on Brian sipping tea from a white mug behind it. I hadn't been long in the prison when Brian stopped me clanging up the metal stairs to the hospital landing. When he asked my name & I said I was Mrs McGlinchey. I heard sniggering voices repeating, *Mrs McGlinchey!* A woman officer roared from the landing above, *Watch out for Brian, he's a pervert!* Eyes darted from the cages all around & Justin's eyes were running like black tar in here, too, telling me *I* was the pervert so eager to tell Brian my name.

KEEP YOUR MIND ON THE JOB AND YOUR EYE ON THE ROAD. ANTICIPATE TROUBLE.

40.

'No, no,' he said; 'you must not walk here; the dogs are too fierce.'

A WEEK later, Brian called *Mrs McGlinchey!* down a metal staircase & I heard the sniggers again. Where were the noises coming from? So many people were hanged or hanged themselves in here. I couldn't get Madame Tussauds' sickly waxworks out of my mind. Or the body of the inventor of the All-Seeing Panopticon Eye, Jeremy Bentham, stuffed & preserved like a pickle & stored in a cupboard in UCL. Dora wouldn't allow me mention Bentham while she was still recovering from Utilitarianism. Brian looked a off-white waxwork too, determinedly sipping tea behind the black door. I was determined too, determined to get away from him. I dropped all the X-ray forms on the floor & when he helped me to pick them up, our heads touched. Back in X-ray, my face reddened, I slammed the door & leant against the wall, I felt the wooden X-ray screen. Wasn't it light? Where was the lead?

ALWAYS LOOK BEFORE YOU OPEN A DOOR.

41.

What do you think of that? he asked as he stood back and folded his arms.

WHEN I asked Mr Barnsley about radiation protection for prisoners, he looked at me. Criminality was genetic, better if they were sterilised – was his opinion & Dora said, *What about yourself? If the equipment is condemned & not good for them*, *what's it doing to you? You could be a red-hot rasher yourself.* & I said, *But it's invisible. I don't know.* Brian arrived with the first prisoner, still holding the white mug. *I wouldn't have it on my conscience. You shouldn't be on your own. Would you like a cup of tea?* he asked, as if there wasn't a heaving list & a load of prisoners in grey trackies thrown into the holding cell, all arms & legs, like crabs in a bucket. I said I never had tea at Pentonville & he asked how long I'd been coming. *Ten and a half months. And no one has asked you in all that time if you'd like a cup of tea? In ten and a half months? I am very upset to hear that,* said Brian.

TO ASSIST YOU WITH THE ABOVE IT WILL BE NECESSARY TO LEARN THE RULES AND CUSTOMS OF THE ESTABLISHMENT.

42.

There is reason that all things are as they are, and did you see with my eyes and know with my knowledge, you would perhaps better understand.

SUTTON, the first prisoner, white as paper, clutched the left side of his chest, black fingernails buried in his grey T-shirt. *What's today's date? Is it the fifteenth? Yes,* said Brian. *Twenty-fourth anniversary of decimalisation in Britain!* I looked at him. *It's the day after Valentine's, that's how I remember it.* Behind the screen, I told Brian that I worried about Sutton. *His colour is desperate, he can hardly stand! Yes, he is generally this colour most of the time,* said Brian. *Maybe he needs a dose of cod liver oil.* Before I went into the dark room, I said it again. *He doesn't look right* & Brian said, *He's been like that for some time now.* The next patient was called James Last. He put his hand up, *I've heard all the jokes!* But I never laughed at people's names, only once when I X-rayed William Shakespeare in the Mater, Dublin. He was so insulted, he didn't speak to me for the rest of the X-ray.

WARNING SIGNS GIVE ADVANCE WARNING OF A HAZARD. THEY ARE IN BLACK AND YELLOW.

43.

Quicker and quicker danced the dust; the moonbeams seemed to quiver as they went by me into the mass of gloom beyond.

JAMES Last had worked with asbestos. *I'll be interested to see his X-rays,* Brian followed me into the dark-room, standing beside me as we peered up through the drips at the film held against the red safelights. *What are you looking for?* asked Brian & I said I was going to ask *him* what *he* was looking for. *What does asbestosis look like on an X-ray?* I wasn't going mention shaggy heart syndrome with Brian standing so close. *Like a silvery honeycomb?* I said doubtfully & Brian said I made it sound very romantic. *Is the heart enlarged?* he asked & I said it looked normal. *Anyway he hasn't got it,* I said & gave the radiograph a hard shake over his shoes. *Hasn't got what?* he skipped to one side. *Asbestosis,* I said & asked him how many more patients because I was desperate for him to go. *Guess what I am in for?* shouted James Last from the X-ray table. *I couldn't possibly,* I said.

CARE SHOULD BE TAKEN WHEN TALKING WITHIN EARSHOT OF INMATES.

44.

*And so you, like the others, would play your brains against mine.
You would help these men to hunt me and frustrate me in my designs!*

DRUNKEN *Driving, Imagine it! He's with us for ten weeks only,* said Brian as if James Last really was a celebrity. Last had been already off the road when he was forced to drive after his mate Darren ate some bad cockles in Southend. Darren, so sick his face *was red as a burst tomato. I only drove 800 yards. Stupid!* he said. But how was he spotted on so short a journey? *Aren't they bang slap outside the pubs now just waiting to pounce?* said Brian in an insulted voice. *They're hunting us down!* said Last & then interrupted himself to say he'd installed computer systems *World-wide!* & if anyone asked him was he British, he said no, he was Cockney & the Cockneys came to London from Norfolk hundreds of years ago looking for work & brought their *funny accents with them.* Brian put down his white mug & folded his black-sleeved arms to listen, happy as man in a dream.

*THE ONLY SAFE RULE IS:
IF YOU DRIVE, DON'T DRINK
IF YOU DRINK, DON'T DRIVE.*

45.

Arthur held out his hand, and took the old man's warmly. 'Call me what you will,' he said.

DR HAND, the junior doctor who never wanted trouble, called Brian out, *Just for a minute I promise!* Brian said, *You'll be safe with James Last, He's a good man, he's a cleaner.* Last laughed, *the good prisoners get to do all the work!* Lying on his left side while I was developing his lateral lumbar spine he shouted, *I decided to get a full check-up while I was at it! You're just lucky you're getting out!* I said, thinking of Sutton, white as a vampire, his pupils like pin-pricks. Brian came back & said we had three more so I tried to speed up but Brian would not rush. *Meet Tiny,* he said, clasping a tall dark man by his red armband. *He's a Red Band,* said Brian. *What's a Red Band? They get to go outside the barbed wire and sweep the car park.* I asked why & Brian said because they were *very well-behaved. Red Bands aren't married either,* said Tiny & winked at me.

YOU SHOULD NOT SHOW FAVOURITISM TO ANY INMATE.

46.

... had he power to move himself as he wished he could go either as man, or wolf, or bat, or in some other way...

I GO *shopping and everything,* said Tiny. *On Roman Way?* I asked & Tiny said he was only joking. *Why are you inside if you're so good? Stupid isn't it? What's stupid ?* I said. Tiny said he thought I knew. & then I had a sinking feeling that I *did* know. *I'd six pints. It was Christmas. First offence,* butted in Brian, *hunted down while real criminals are out robbing all round.* Were the drunken drivers his pets? Everyone's pets with their Red Bands & special duties? So eager to tell me their not crimes. I never asked why they were in but these ones *wanted* me to know. My eyes filled with tears. Silvery glints flittered in the air. Brian & Tiny smiled. Did they think I was crying for Tiny? *If your wife was in labour would they put you inside?* I asked, remembering Carl driving Red Astra round the Whittington car park, jaunty & confused asking me where he could park an hour before Baby was born.

REMEMBER THAT EVEN A SMALL AMOUNT OF ALCOHOL WILL SLOW YOUR REACTIONS AND AFFECT YOUR SKILL

47.

Then, amongst a chorus of screams from the peasants and a universal crossing of themselves, a calèche, with four horses, drove up behind us.

LISTEN, said Tiny. *There's a fellow down there & he was driving his sick son to the hospital!* Brian nodded as I remembered the accidents in the early hours, the sickening smell of blood & alcohol. Moving the ceiling-mounted X-ray tube around the blood-stained bodies in their stiff white collars, holding my breath as I pressed the exposure button. Legs missing, necks broken, my own neck whipping back & forth in the concertina'd white Escort on the Stillorgan Dual Carriageway. Brian said that the law was *an ass, you could be in prison for selling a postage stamp on a Sunday outside of a post office. If I needed a postage stamp on a Sunday & you sold me one you'd be breaking the law.* When McCarthy staggered in, I knew by the way his wrist was hanging, it was broken. *It has been like that for two weeks now,* Brian lowered his voice, watching my face.

INMATES SHOULD NOT HEAR CONFIDENTIAL INFORMATION ABOUT THEMSELVES OR STAFF.

48.

They learned his secrets in the Scholomance, amongst the mountains over Lake Hermanstadt, where the devil claims the tenth scholar as his due.

BEFORE I left, Brian said I was a *very caring & professional worker* & I wondered what he was up to because I was thirty-three & could not be taken in any more. He came back again & said *Be sure and call me, shout for Brian if you ever need a cup of tea.* While I was writing up the envelopes, there was the loudest shouting I'd ever heard in the prison. SIT DOWN! SIT DOWN! SIT DOWN! I waited for the alarm to go off but it didn't & I walked through the prison, Fierce Annoyed that they thought I was crying for fucking Tiny. Was it a delayed reaction to the shock of Carl losing his licence? Which I must never mention. No one must know why I was suddenly Behind the Wheel. Carl had his own Official Secrets Act & even though he said he was being ironic when he played Tammy singing *Stand by Your Man,* I wasn't when I played my favourite, *Our D.I.V.O.R.C.E. becomes final today.*

SIGNAL YOUR INTENTION TO MOVE OUT.

49.

...the wonderful smoky beauty of a sunset over London, with its lurid lights and inky shadows and all the marvellous tints that come on foul clouds...

I TURNED the key in Red Astra & Linton said, *Inglan is a Bitch. He* wouldn't stand around nodding & smiling, tears in his eyes pretending to agree with everyone. They thought I was a 'nice' girl. Mr Barnsley couldn't believe that I'd ever smoked. One white-sleeved arm shot to his head in the red glow of the dark room & we were only talking about cigs. I hated going round like a Holy Mary. Sometimes I was *called* Mary if people didn't know my name & if I said it was racist, they thought it was Fierce Funny. Irish people were just funny until they just weren't, like Oscar Wilde. When I walked back through the yard, the blue sky made everything worse. The sky was so noticeable inside. I thought again of the 'little piece of blue' in *The Ballad of Reading Gaol.* My key clattered back down the chute, a Dulux lorry was leaving. No colours in the prison looked anything like the side of that van.

BE AWARE OF THE IMPORTANCE OF NOT LEAVING YOUR PLACE OF WORK WITHOUT INFORMING YOUR COLLEAGUES.

50.

There must be a transfusion of blood at once. Is it you or me?

WEDNESDAY mornings were a relief when they arrived becau waiting was worse. I left early so there was time to let cars tur right if they had to & for me to turn right too. *Jesus, will you s doing that!* Carl said. *But someone has to let them in, they can't stay there forever. And if two people insist, won't there be a crash?* Carl jerked in the passenger seat like he really was riding shotgun but he still said I was *great at the driving!* once we were out of the car. Inside, he shuddered & pointed in directions that were hard to follow, shouting *Now! Now! Over There! Watch it!* I dreaded the giant sprawl where Camden Park Road met York Way, straining for Market Road. How I could get past all those red-hot right-turning cars. Then one morning worrying about why Dr Cherry hadn't mentioned the union letter I turned right in front of a black cab. Did I see a terrified face in the mirror as I drove away?

ALWAYS CONSULT YOUR MIRROR BEFORE YOU OVERTAKE, SLOW DOWN, STOP OR OPEN THE DOOR.

51.

…it did not seem a short time either, for the draining away of one's blood, no matter how willingly it be given, is a terrible feeling…

ON Roman Way, my suede toe touched a bright red King of Diamonds card on the pavement, navy-blue eyes like Dr Grey. Who genuinely thought I was to be accompanied in X-ray but now made jokes like he was a Tough Guy. *You have to do what they ask for in here!* I stopped at the corner shop to buy newspapers for the dark room floor – to keep my heels from skidding in the pools of chemicals. Customers queued dreamily for scratch cards as if there weren't a thousand prisoners fit to burst behind the wall on the other side of the road. My charcoal toes were worn, I needed new shoes. Soon the MOT would be due & I would have to drive all the way to Fortune Green Road! *Pack Red Astra* said Dora *& drive off with your books & Baby* but *driving off* anywhere was the last thing I wanted to do & besides Red Astra was a company car.

SIGNAL CLEARLY, DECISIVELY AND IN GOOD TIME.

52.

I agree that there has been much blood lost…

HE *doesn't feel sorry for* you, said Dora. *But I promised to go back for good,* I said. *And you've done ten years! He knows Justin. They trapped you.* I saw a cow, running to mart before a stick. Justin always took care of the drinkers. Agnes said he was *too soft, too good!* He said it himself, a Bloody Mary in his sallow hand, black head lit up by the lights behind the upside-down whiskey bottles, Jameson, Powers, Paddy. *Too fucking good. Should let them all drink themselves to death instead of wasting my time feeding them coffee & ham sandwiches.* Clodagh buttered their bread with Blue Band margarine. *For the heart!* John Twohig sat white & shivering at the counter, his long skinny legs entwining the black legs of the bar stool. *Putty in my hands!* said Justin. *Poor Marian at home,* said Agnes. *Oh the lies! the lies out of them! You can't beat an alcoholic for lies,* Justin drained his ruby-red glass.

REMEMBER THAT EVEN A SMALL AMOUNT OF ALCOHOL WILL SLOW YOUR REACTIONS AND AFFECT YOUR SKILL.

53.

'Take care,' he said, 'take care how you cut yourself. It is more dangerous than you think in this country.'

JOHN Twohig's Marian said at his funeral that she'd *do it all again. Is it better to say that than to admit you've been had?* I asked & Agnes said I had a depressing outlook. *She adored him!* What was there to adore in a grey corpse in love with itself & no pity for anyone else? Night after night, the late return, *I just dropped into The Crown & a Cork crowd wouldn't let go of me until I'd sung every verse of the Boston Burglar.* The professions of love, the vomiting, the tormenting. I vomited too, hit him to keep him away. *You were dying for it in your sleep.* But I only remembered dreams of people turning over three times in their cars. Sometimes I dreamt I was on call & the phone wouldn't stop ringing. I told them, *I'm coming*! but went back to sleep & they rang again. *Didn't you sound so sweet and obliging?* Sister White said. *We're outside with the stretcher. Open that door & get me a lead apron!*

WHAT TYPES AND WHERE ARE THE FIRE FIGHTING APPLIANCES FOR YOUR WORK AREA?

54.

I knew the man by the neck and the movement of his back and arms.

THAT smell of blood & alcohol. Carl unsteady on the stairs, black & white outraged face, waving the clear plastic bag with his bunches of keys & his wallet & all the black & silvery things inside. I looked down at the unconscious body on the table, scabs already forming on the face framed in the stiff white collar. *I suppose you get away with murder, doing the sweet act,* says Sister White. *Well, I wasn't really awake,* I said & gave her heaviest lead apron, the grey one. Date of birth: June 10, '74. *Driver's crying his eyes out down in casualty & he hasn't a scratch.* Pulling down the X-ray tube, balancing the cassette between his ear & his shoulder with the tomato-red bottle of developer & a sandbag. Sister White's elbows on the tall film processor, its heat drew us like an open fire. Young bones gleamed like ivory in the dark viewing area. A very pretty picture – I could see as far as T2. *His neck is broken,* I said.

IN DENSE FOG, USE YOUR DIPPED HEADLAMPS,
AND FOLLOW THE LEFT-HAND KERB.

55.

There was a full moonlight, and I could see that the noise was made by a great bat, which wheeled round – doubtless attracted by the light…

SOME alcoholics had such glamour. Was that what got me? Every woman loves the Nazi boot, said Sylvia matching Oscar's *Every man kills the thing he loves.* Justin talked of alcoholics like he was observing wild creatures. *The lies! Oh, the lies out of them!* *But surely,* I asked. *Not all of them?* Ould Jack came to the shop with a plastic bag, *There is my sack, give me a brack*, went into the bar, ordered a pint & only opened his mouth to swallow after that, pointing once to the glass every time it emptied. He plámásed no one, took his brack in his sack, went out in the black night. Sometimes he fell down like a stone in the ditch & no one knew how he wasn't killed on the road with *half of them over the limit*, Justin said. *But that's alcoholics, they're like vampires you can't kill them.* Justin drained his Bloody Mary. His long black hair, pale yellow face, black eyes in Clodagh's grey velvet jacket. *So sad*, Agnes said.

TAKE EXTRA CARE ON COUNTRY ROADS AND REDUCE YOUR SPEED AT APPROACHES TO BENDS, WHICH CAN BE SHARPER THAN THEY APPEAR.

56.

It was half-past two o'clock when the knock came…

THE glamour overwhelmed us. Mrs Burke-White in a silver dress, pink bows on her shoulders, her white-blonde hair reflected in the huge gilt mirror over the bar fireplace, singing *I Feel Pretty, Witty and Gay,* eyes on Justin as he stirred another Bloody Mary. She'd been on the Late Late Show talking about tidiness. Her big tip? *Pick up as you go along!* said Clodagh as if anyone needed that advice with Justin so desperate tidy. Going round the pool table with a big ruler, measuring strips for protecting the carpet in the New Lounge. Cutting the red & black lino exactly along the lines of the check, lips sharp as the Stanley knife in his hand. *Her voice is like a silver bell,* Clodagh said & I heard again the 2.30 a.m. knocks on the hall door, *Justin! Justin McConnell! Open up! We are after turning over three times on the road outside Whitechurch.*

BE PREPARED FOR PEDESTRIANS, HORSE RIDERS, CYCLISTS, SLOW-MOVING FARM VEHICLES OR MUD ON THE ROAD SURFACE.

57.

I make pretty wreath, and hang him round your neck, so that you sleep well.

BRANDY was called for – *Oh Fill Up Once More,* sang Granddad cynically next morning, tapping the red Formica table in the kitchen. *That white dress with the black patent belt* said Clodagh. *Six inches deep! But she could carry anything off. Even after an accident.* Granddad's crooked fingers danced on the pattern of fawn twigs on the cochineal Formica. I got lost staring at the twigs, searched for years for the end to the thread. *Oh Fill Up Once More,* Granddad sang again. *To Dear Old Erin's Isle,* Clodagh answered in her glassy voice, patting his hand. *Her lofty banks, her… what's next?* Granddad looked at her, *Sure that's all wrong! Oh is it? Maybe you're right,* she said in a sweet voice. Was she turning into Agnes? Was I? Was that what Sister White meant when she said I answered the call from Casualty *so sweetly,* going back to sleep while an 18-year-old lay outside X-ray with a broken neck.

MAKE ALLOWANCES FOR OTHER ROAD USERS, EVEN THOSE WHO FAIL TO SHOW GOOD MANNERS AND SENSE.

58.

Remember that he has the strength of twenty men, and that, though our necks or our windpipes are of the common kind – and therefore breakable or crushable – his are not amenable to mere strength

WHY didn't the people from my childhood break their necks? Or maybe they did & it was an Official Secrets Act. People seemed to be always turning over three times on the road or was that a figure of speech to express the relief & guilt when they walked away without a scratch? *But she was in a terrible state,* said Justin. *& Father Dunne too, they were coming home from a music rehearsal. At two in the morning!* said Granddad, his fingertips black from turning the pages of *The Cork Examiner*. *Father Dunne is dapper, isn't he*? said Clodagh. *Wasn't his houndstooth waistcoat handsome! That was his costume*, said Justin, *the man was in shock. Shock, is it?* said Granddad, *Smiling at himself in the hallstand & tap dancing into the bathroom. Was it a musical number?* I asked & Granddad shuddered when I sang *Ooh Oklahoma! where the wind comes sweepin' down the plains! Ah Jaysus*, he said & put his crooked hands over his ears.

IF YOU DO GET INTO A SKID, KEEP COOL AND DO NOT USE THE CLUTCH OR APPLY THE BRAKES.

59.

The decanter of sherry was on the table half full, but there was a queer, acrid smell about.

SOME people – & all surgeons – were allowed to roar as much as they liked, along with many alcoholics because people – often women – thought they were *so sad*. Mick got away with roaring too & the sad thing was I did think he was *so sad*. Carl had been *so sad* too, my tears a blood transfusion for him until I dried up completely. I asked after Mick's cat Prince & Mick said Prince was *Top of the Pops!* He was red-eyed & groaning himself, the grey end of his fag glowing crimson as he puffed it in and out – on & off like the X-ray warning light – *Haven't touched a drink for two weeks, 'Melda!* or *three months since a drop passed these lips* or simply – *nothing since last Tuesday* & saying this on Wednesday morning. I bumped into him on Holloway Road, his foot on the threshold of The Cock Tavern. He said he was there to see the GAA matches in colour because he only had a black & white TV.

AT ALL TIMES BE ON THE ALERT FOR CARELESS PEDESTRIANS.

60.

I was suspicious and examined the decanter.

WHEN I asked Mick about Rachel Hatred he said he was talking about the Jamaican porters who were *hogging all the overtime.* But they brought the patients down when they were asked & were Fierce Crack. I imagined them splitting their sides at Mick's roars, his face red as a boiled prawn under his wobbling Mr Whippy combover. He said they left him with all the morgue stuff. *But you love the morgue!* I said.
He said he'd run away from an undertaking family in Borris-in-Ossory when he was young but the work stayed in his blood. *Dead babies are the worst,* he said. *To see those families crying and mauling the body!* His carmine trainers from another jumble sale, squeaked on the grey lino. He lifted one glowing foot, *How much do you think, 'Melda?* I hoped he didn't hiss in the background when the relatives were looking at the babies.

BE AWARE OF OTHER STAFF NEEDS AND PROVIDE ADEQUATE SUPPORT IN ANY SITUATION.

61.

The Count's mysterious warning frightened me at the time; it frightens me more now when I think of it...

GRANDDAD said Mrs Burke-White was in *a woeful state, screeching inside in the bathroom,* leaving red toothy lipstick marks all over the towel. *I knew white towels were a mistake*! said Clodagh. *I should have gone for the geranium-red.* Granddad saw Mrs Burke-White through the half-open door, hanging on to the washstand. *That's the shock,* said Clodagh. & Granddad said she was laughing her head off, singing into the mirror – *I've been a wild rover for many a year!* Justin turned over on the road three times too. Was *three times turnover* code for *Big Fright?* St Paul on the road to Damascus? Carl'd seen *a light* the night he was arrested. Could it be the light Hank Williams saw when *Jesus came like a stranger in the night?* & Hank died in his car in mysterious circumstances. Carl cried when he saw Baby the day after. But at the same time, *those fucking anti-Irish police.*

THE DIAGRAM IS BASED ON THE ASSUMPTION THAT THE DRIVER APPLIES HIS BRAKES IN AN EMERGENCY IN TWO THIRDS OF A SECOND AND ON A DRY LEVEL ROAD SURFACE.

62.

after a little play back and forward the bolt yielded, and, with a rusty clang, shot back.

THE usual Gate was *not operational* because of construction works. Still worried about no response to the union letter I walked to the huge octagonal cream gates breaking the wall on Caledonian Road, rang the bell. A dark-eyed officer looked out the slit window at me. I walked into a huge cage, with a mirror like an operating theatre light stuck to the roof. The gate staff were in a Portakabin. I showed my ID card, my keys clattered into the iron chute & the racket began. Prisoners banged into their cells, clanking of chains & keys & gates & alarms. Officers stood round wearing their coats. It was freezing & the rain came down in cold whips as I ran through the cage in my thin black cardigan. *Easy there, partner!* they shouted after me, enjoying my big red face. They had to do a *bag search*. Or at least that's what they said.

EXPECT TO BE REFUSED ENTRY IF YOU CANNOT SHOW YOUR ID CARD.

63.

But as to the odour itself, how shall I describe it? It was not alone that it was composed of all the ills of mortality and with the pungent, acrid smell of blood, but it seemed as though corruption had become itself corrupt. Faugh! it sickens me to think of it.

ANOTHER gate in another cage-wall. I unlocked it. I never could believe how I was let off like that with my bunch of keys. Like a housekeeper from a Victorian novel, like Mrs Fairfax. If I had a rustling crinoline & a big black bonnet it might give me authority. Black uniformed officers dotted the yard, one tawny Alsatian on a leash. A new metal ramp to the hospital side door bypassed the main prison. Yet another gate & a heavy wooden door to unlock & then the smell hit me for the fiftieth time. What made it? Was it dirt? Unwashed bodies? It had a horrible smoothness which I couldn't place & yet it was pungent, catching the back of my throat. To the left, the kitchens, trolley, food containers stacked up. Two Prison Officers stood beside the food like black shadows. They didn't say hello so I didn't bother either. Was I on a blacklist?

SHOW YOUR ID CARD EACH TIME YOU COME INTO THE ESTABLISHMENT. NOT ALL STAFF ON THE GATE CAN BE EXPECTED TO KNOW YOU.

64.

He was lying on his belly on the floor licking up, like a dog, the blood which had fallen from my wounded wrist.

CARL had wondered if they had me *marked* the week before & I said I couldn't take any more Terror & he said that I couldn't be too careful with an Irish accent & the Prevention of Terrorism Act. & *bringing in the union.* I asked him if he'd been talking to Justin & he said he was talking to *me* & that Socialism & Sinn Féin were as one. *It wouldn't be the first time they banged up a Red Mick. And what about Mad Dog McGlinchy?* Carl worried they'd think we were related. *They'll be after me next!* he said & I said *Who is they?* feeling fierce guilty for bringing trouble to our door until I spoke to Dora who got hopping mad, *Well, why doesn't he let you leave the prison so? I don't know which one of you is worse – Carl for issuing orders or you for taking them. But he doesn't like my determined jaw,* I said. *Well, at least stop bleeding in front of him, he's lapping it up. The enemy is within!* But within who, I wondered.

REGULATORY SIGNS IMPLEMENT ROAD REGULATIONS AND SHOW THE COURSE TO FOLLOW, ETC. THE COLOUR RED IS USED TO COMMAND ATTENTION.

65.

Into two of these I went, but saw nothing except fragments… and piles of dust…

AFTER I arrived at the clinic, I was glad to see the Fierce Nice young officer I'd worked with once before. Quite heavy & strong-looking with a spiky fair fringe. She'd got all my stuff from the office, everything ready. Usually I was lucky if they even had the key of the X-ray door which I collected now, clattering off in my scuffed shoes to the X-ray room. As I entered the dark room, I caught my breath at the shapes of four grey child-sized coffins on the floor but when I turned on the light, they were just cases made of stiff heavy card marked DENTAL RECORDS. No one knew what they were doing in the dark room & I couldn't lift them. I had to ask the Clinic to remove them on top of everything else. Boxes of Kodak & chemicals in Pharmacy, waiting to be delivered & two lead-heavy piles of X-rays to go down to Stores. I tried not to ask for too much at once.

REFUSE MUST BE DISPOSED OF IN THE PROPER MANNER FOR THE ITEMS CONCERNED.

66.

For he suddenly grew pale and sat down in a chair almost fainting…

FIRST patient – O'Toole was young & Irish with two silver flashing earrings. Too sick to even ask me what county I was from. I X-rayed his shoulder & his foot which dripped sweat in a continuous stream. There was something really wrong with him. Swollen-faced Witcher needed a mandible. Beaten up by another prisoner. Or was he? Then Scrubbs, sullen, holding his left hand in a dramatic clasp, fuck all wrong with him, followed by Quinn – Irish again – for a chest. Earl came after Quinn, sporting a red bracelet. Hardly a Red Band? He didn't have the Red Band air of being pure delighted with himself. He fidgeted with his grey sweatshirt when I asked him to lie on the table. I wished I could ask him what *he* thought of Red Bands as I slid the cassette under his knee warning him it was cold. What did I know, my visits so short & fierce? Undercover my eye. I was peering through a keyhole full of smoke.

LOOK IN THE MIRROR FROM TIME TO TIME.

67.

I tried to be stern with him, as one is to a woman under the circumstances; but it had no effect.

I CAME out of the dark room & told Earl I'd have to do another X-ray. A skyline view of the patella. *Just to be sure your kneecap is okay.* He'd been lying flat & then he sprang into a sitting position, put his hands up to the tube head. I'd never seen a patient lay hands on an X-ray tube before. He began to stroke it as if he was playing a harp, looking at me, seeing how far he could go. He knew he was funny. Like Chaplin holding the globe, pretending to be Hitler. I bit my cheek, struck by this show with an audience of one in the dim grey X-ray room buried in the hospital inside the prison. Was he ok though? *We're all mad here!* I wanted to say. Then he stopped abruptly, *Are you irradiating me? Well, I have to use radiation to get an X-ray,* I said, *but it's only for point zero two of a second. Point zero two of a second!* he laughed & lay down again. *I am your prisoner!*

IT IS IMPERATIVE THAT STAFF SHOULD NOT LOSE SIGHT OF THE HUMAN ELEMENT IN THEIR CONTACTS WITH PRISONERS AND SHOULD RECOGNISE THE SIGNS OF BOREDOM, ANXIETY, INCOMPATIBILITY WITH OTHER PRISONERS OR INABILITY TO ACCEPT THE PRISON REGIME ARE OFTEN INDICATIONS THAT AN INDIVIDUAL MAY BREACH SECURITY IN SOME WAY.

68.

As I appeared they all joined in a horrible laugh and ran away.

IN the clinic office, a white-haired officer raged, *How incompetent stupid and inept can this place get? You'll never guess what? Locke has been sent on a personal training course! &* they all said how slimy, useless, slippery, pushy, tale-telling & slimy Locke was. The Irish PSN said he was *like slapping KY jelly against your hand* which I found hard to imagine. After I'd X-rayed three, Pam – an officer with a chopped black fringe – appeared & said there were seven more & I said I'd never get them done on time for Dr Grey. They'd have to go back. *You'll do what you're told,* she said & came back with a man called Jimmy Ash who said, *But it's an eye test I need! Where?* I asked. *On the outside,* he eyed me, hopefully as if I'd take him with me. Then Pam said *none* of the seven were for X-ray & I was released. I sang *look out! & I did warn yu!* tidying the dark room in the red glow of the safelights.

BE AWARE OF OTHER STAFF NEEDS AND PROVIDE ADEQUATE SUPPORT IN ANY SITUATION.

69.

I ran to the door, intending to descend and try and join them…
Again a shock: my door was fastened on the outside.

BUT Pam came back again & said there were seven in another holding cell. I did Murphy's toe & sent the rest of them back. Everyone was sullen in the office even my fair spiky-haired friend when I left at 11.45 a.m. I wished Dr Grey'd arrived at 10.50 a.m. as he said he would. He was the one who said the X-rays had to be done or sent back by 11.15. Now it looked like – & I could see that they wanted to believe – I was just *pissing off early* in a high-handed way. Maybe even *flouncing*? Maybe I, too, was *just like KY jelly slapped against your hand.* If only Dr Grey would come in & dazzle us all in his white coat to save my reputation but he never did. As I walked along Roman Way like a drowned vinegary rat to Red Astra, two mounted policemen passed on black & white horses. Even the horses looked disgusted after two seconds of inspecting me with their black, white & red watery eyes.

DO NOT LOITER ON THE ROADWAY.

70.

I start at my own shadow, and am full of all sorts of horrible imaginings.

ON Brecknock Road a dark Saab flashed its lights behind me.
Last time a car flashed its lights at me, it was a police car near
Tollington Way. I'd flashed mine back warmly, thinking it was
letting me through. Even dared to lift one hand from the wheel
to reinforce my gratitude with a wave before it chased me
to Baby's nursery on Stapleton Hall Road, blue light on.
The policeman said he'd been warning me *not* to turn left
(or was it right?) into empty Bavaria Road where I'd felt so safe.
You could have three points on your licence, he said as I leant against
Red Astra because my legs wouldn't support me. *Think you can
charm your way through life with one wave of your hand?* & it'd been
such an effort to make that wave. Now my whiplashed neck
grated like Styrofoam. I couldn't feel the pedals. The Saab beeped.
I pulled over to let it go but it pulled up right behind me.

USE THE HORN, WITH DISCRETION AND CONSIDERATION FOR OTHERS, AS A WARNING AND NOT AS A THREAT.

71.

...the thick eyebrows that met over the nose now seemed like a heaving bar of white-hot metal.

WAS it the undercover police? He looked like a banker in a crisp shirt, sleeves rolled up, black & red Rolex on his gold arm. He gestured & I pressed the button to lower the window. *Do me a favour & read the bloody Rules of the Road!* he roared in at me. *I will!* I said. *I'm on my way home & I'll do it immediately!* He jumped like he was stung, his eyes glistening, *Smart, are you? No, I am not!* What could I say to make him go? His crisp shirt. Disgusted tanned face, staring in at me, nearly fainting in my seat. Was he going to drag me out? *I really want to read the Rules of the Road, I swear!* I said & then he looked sorry, his eyes travelling over my white uniform as I cowered in my stains. When he walked away, I wondered if it was the developer smell that saved me. He was fit to burst as a prisoner. But why did *he* get to roar? Patrick Allbrow had to bottle it up.

A DRIVER NEEDS TO BE ABLE TO JUDGE A SAFE SEPARATION DISTANCE AT ALL TIMES.

72.

...a dog began to howl somewhere in a farmhouse far down the road...

ALLBROW was a real Dub. A Northsider. Wiry, with a thin red scar curved around his chin. He'd been hospitalised as a child but he couldn't remember which one. *Mercy maybe?* he said & I wondered if it was Mercer's Hospital. *That's the one!* he said. *At the top of Grafton Street?* I said. *That's the one!* I wasn't sure at first if he wasn't just agreeing with me. They often took their cue from me. Like Earweather who said he'd an old knee injury & when I asked him – what I didn't realise were leading questions – he ended up saying he'd had his knee cap severed. His X-ray didn't show the smallest sign of an old injury. Patients on the outside rarely did this. But Patrick Allbrow sagged when he heard Mercer's was closed, only cheered up when I said I trained with a girl whose mother'd been a radiographer at Mercer's. *Did she talk about it often?* he asked.

ALL THE RULES FOR GOOD ROAD BEHAVIOUR COULD BE SUMMED UP IN TWO: TAKE CARE. SHOW CONSIDERATION FOR OTHERS.

73.

I have been since yesterday in a sort of fever of doubt…

ALLBROW *is a funny name for an Irishman! Well, I'm Irish anyway my father came from Cork. West Cork. I can't remember where, I was back there for a funeral once.* The form said he'd had *a bit of an infection.* Dr Grey recommended a follow-up. The follow-up always caused so much worry. He was in a state & I couldn't tell him why because of confidentiality. He worried about cancer & he wasn't sleeping. *I'd be the same,* I said *but I am not worried about you!* I asked if the doctor had given any antibiotics, thinking he'd say yes & then I could say the X-ray was to check his chest was clearing. *No, I didn't get any antibiotics*, he said & gave me a wild look, the whites of his eyes threaded with red. *I haven't even spoken to a doctor. Have you been coughing up stuff?* I asked. *No!* he looked wilder. *I've got an awful pain on the right side of my chest. I find it hard to get my breath.*

REMEMBER THAT FOG CAN DRIFT RAPIDLY AND IS OFTEN PATCHY.

74.

His face was deathly pale…

AFTER I'd seen the X-ray & it really did look clearer – (within reason because it was dripping all over the place, including into my eyes) – I told him *definitely not to worry*. I wanted to reassure patients & I so rarely could. *I'm not qualified to give out the results*, you had to be emphatic, unapproachable. Like steel. I wasn't & they knew. *But you'd know anyway, wouldn't you?* They twisted the knife. A nervous man came into the Whittington for a chest X-ray & said, *I know if you send me away, there's nothing wrong with my chest!* When I was sending him away, he roared above the grey drowsing bodies in the waiting room, *I know I'm normal! You wouldn't send me away, would you, if I wasn't normal?* To take Patrick's mind off his chest I asked him about Mercer's again. He said he was in Mercer's for a long time when he was a child. For asthma & double-pneumonia. *I didn't want to come home at the end of the seven years!*

EVEN IF IT SEEMS TO BE CLEARING, YOU CAN SUDDENLY FIND YOURSELF BACK IN THICK FOG.

75.

In the old days there were stirring times...

WHEN Patrick's aunt came for him, he went under the bed, she had to hold a half crown to get him out. He loved one nurse, *She was very good to me, god, she was nice too!* Once when he was bold, she tried to catch hold of him & scratched his face. *Drew blood! She didn't mean it, you know it was my fault for being a blackguard. But Jesus when I think of it, I could have sued her or anything.* He stopped & looked at me, his scar livid. Maybe I could be sued too? I went red. In Mercer's, he could look out & see his mother in the street below, working her stall outside the hospital. *Like Molly Malone wheeling her barrow through streets broad & narrow. Cockles & Mussels!* I was glad he only sang for a minute. His sisters had the stall now, they'd moved to Great George's Street. He was chirpy at the end, hoping he wouldn't see me in the X-ray room again. *I wouldn't mind outside of it though!*

REMEMBER THAT ON GUSTY DAYS A CYCLIST IS LIABLE TO BE BLOWN OFF COURSE.

76.

... when he found that his appeal would not be successful, he got into quite a frantic condition.

I X-RAYED Brown the same day, his fourth knuckle puffed up – a crimson balloon. They were looking for glass in the wound. He'd been taken to an outside hospital to get his injured hand treated. I couldn't find out the original problem but he tried to do a runner, put his hand *straight through* a plate glass window. He sighed continuously & didn't take his tired pink eyes from his enormous red knuckle, just kept asking me if he'd be sent outside for an operation. Then Tidy, one of the officers from the hospital came in & asked for a look at the X-ray. Tidy liked to give the impression he knew what he was looking at. His bouffant glam rock haircut made him look younger at a distance but up close, his hair was dusted with grey & two lines ran straight down from the corners of his mouth. I couldn't see any glass in Brown's finger. *It doesn't always show,* I said. *I know that!* Tidy said.

ALL INMATES SHOULD BE RUB-DOWN SEARCHED BEFORE BEING MOVED FROM ONE AREA TO ANOTHER.

77.

Oh, my friend John, but it was butcher work…

HE's *anxious to have an operation. Will he be going outside?* Tidy looked scoffingly into my eyes. *Oh he'll be having an op all right. Downstairs with Dr Cherry. Have you got an anaesthetist? Brown won't be needing any anaesthetist. He'll be getting a needle from Dr Cherry & Brown's well used to shoving needles up himself.* Dr Cherry came to look at the X-ray, rubbing his hands behind Brown's back, laughing with Tidy. I felt sick. I wrote Brown's details & asked for his prison number. He groaned, his boiling red hand to his head. It looked so sore & he couldn't remember. Dr Cherry told him to pull himself together. *PA 1234,* ventured Brown. *PA1234?* Tidy must've spent ages, practising his sardonic eyebrows. They hovered above us all as Tidy & Brown settled on a compilation of the numbers. Later I saw his notes by chance. A different number. The notes said he was schizophrenic.

VULNERABLE PRISONERS – THESE INMATES ARE SEGREGATED FROM THE REST OF THE PRISON POPULATION FOR THEIR OWN PROTECTION (NOT DUE TO THE NATURE OF THEIR OFFENCE). THEY MUST BE ESCORTED SEPARATE FROM OTHER PRISONERS.

78.

On a table in the hall was a great bunch of keys, with a time-yellowed label on each…

THE gate reeked of diesel & there was a notice for drivers to check their vehicles for bombs before they left. Who was planting them? From the inside? I could hardly ask now that I was Mrs Mad Dog McGlinchey, chief suspect. I used to think the white uniform was a pure thing, now it was a cursed beacon. If you went to your driving test in a nurse's uniform, you passed automatically, they said. Well, I had to wear it four times & Mr Jones the examiner threw his eyes up every time. Black was better here but they never offered me *their* uniforms. Or much help. An intruder every time I approached the clanging gates, whistles & shouts. No Galway woman today to ask if Baby was over the chickenpox. Another woman, white cup in her cindery, mittened hand, barely nodded. I held my breath against *that* smell, collected my list & X-ray key, Pam seemed friendly for once. Why? I had the key in the door when I saw the notice.

CLINIC OFFICERS ARE NOT EXPECTED TO SIT WITH THE RADIOGRAPHER THROUGH A PROCEDURE BUT WILL GIVE HER ASSISTANCE IN PROMPTLY RESOLVING ANY DIFFICULT SITUATION.

79.

I trust you will forgive me, but I have much work to do in private this evening. You will, I hope, find all things as you wish....

DR CHERRY had typed it on a grey background & black-framed it like a mortuary card. I was to be *made* to work alone. My Styrofoam neck creaked as I ran my eyes down – *1. List of patients… shown to the Radiographer. Health Care Officer to inform Radiographer which patients… Which...order… operational problems. 3… inform clinic staff… procedure completed… patient… promptly returned to the waiting room.* Promptly? Was I hanging on to them? Waiting room? Filthy holding cell! 4. *Clinic officers… not expected to sit with the radiographer… but will give her assistance in promptly...* Where were they when I left the patient in the room, entered the dark room nearly blind because some eedjit had painted it black? They cared less about the radiographers' union. They probably laughed at it. I was on my own. When I asked for Dr Cherry, Pam said he was on holiday. *Burnt out, poor man!* Her eyes knifed me from under the black slash of her fringe.

BE AWARE OF 'BLACK SPOTS'. AREAS OF POOR OR NIL RECEPTION.

80.

So far as I can see, my only plan will be to keep my knowledge and my fears to myself.

I RAN through the noise & smell down the metal staircase to the office. Pam followed, blowing her black fringe like a minotaur, *The radiographer in Brixton X-rays prisoners on his own!* I saw red & spoke back, *I have X-rayed people on my own, miles from casualty in the middle of the night in every hospital ever, I know when I'm not safe. If they follow me into the dark room. I can't be heard if I call for help.* That drove her wild, *Who do you think you are?* she said. *But I was told I'd have someone with me. Mr Barnsley always comes in with me when he's here. Who's* Mister *Barnsley? The tall man from the North of England*, I said & she said, *You're making him up!* So I asked to use the office phone & Carl, finally, after some thinking, agreed I should leave. Too late. Much too late. Dora was right. I'd always been on my own. For now, I practised saying, *My union representative told me not to…*

IN DENSE FOG USE YOUR DIPPED HEADLAMPS AND FOLLOW THE LEFT-HAND KERB.

81.

Do you know where you are going, and what you are going to?

DR HAND waved a white form, asking me to take an X-ray for Dr Jigg. I said I wasn't doing anything *without a member of staff. But this is dreadful!* I knew she didn't want trouble but it was time to make my stand. Another nurse arrived & said Dr Cherry wasn't there as if that settled it. *Wait for him to come back*! *But he's missing because he knows I am about to Make my stand! Your what? My stand! Well put what you're saying in writing!* Dr Hand said. *But my union rep has written to Dr Cherry already! WRITE IT DOWN! WRITE IT DOWN, WRITE IT DOWN!* she raised her flushed voice. Another officer arrived, *the Governor* heard I was leaving & he'd like to see me. *Oh I hear you're leaving!* Mr Baker smirked as if I was a funny nothing. *You have to write it down, you know!* I did after a few false starts & took the letter away to photocopy it. *You have to write it down,* he called after me. *We're sticklers for procedure in the prison service!*

KEEP YOUR MIND ON THE JOB AND YOUR EYE ON THE ROAD. ANTICIPATE TROUBLE.

82.

Raised outcry, and all came on deck…

DR HAND found Brian who came with his tea & stayed while I X-rayed Huston's abdomen. Huston was white as a stick of chalk, his abscess beginning to heal, they were looking for calculi. I couldn't find anything but two silvery eyelets on his shorts that came out magnified. I was not going to ask him take his shorts off. The artefacts were over the pelvis, not in his stomach. Surely they'd figure that out? Brian was icy. Didn't offer me tea & I was tempted to ask for a cup. *Is the door lead-lined?* he asked & I said I'd been wondering the same thing. He looked at me sideways, nervously slurping from his brick-red mug. Huston must've been in terrible pain. Would they even give him painkillers? Dr Jigg wanted the films & I said they were still wet but he could come & look at them in the dark room. Dr Hand was shocked at my *lack of respect* for Dr Jigg. *Yes, the dark room is disgusting!* I said.

DON'T CHANGE YOUR MIND SUDDENLY AND DON'T DITHER.

83.

I had seen that the door was unlocked, and now escape was before me.

DR HAND said she'd look at the films herself & I panicked. Dr Hand thought a perfect C1 looked abnormal. She was relying on me so I said that I couldn't see any calculi. I came out of the office & Mr Barnsley clattered up the metal stairs, *News travels fast!* He wouldn't stay with prisoners on his own if he was a woman, he said & lifted his black strong shoe high above the metal stair tread, *Good to show them who's boss!* Not feeling one bit like a boss or that I was showing anyone anything, I took my photocopied letter back to Mr Baker who was even more cheerful to show me what a relief it was to be rid of me. I caught myself apologising for the grey chemical drips on my letter before I went back to dry my films. Dr Jigg's fastidious white face appeared & disappeared outside the X-ray door for a minute & Pam screeched when I pointed out Mr Barnsley on the stairwell, MISTER *Barnsley! Why can't you call him Keith like everyone else!*

BE AWARE OF OTHER STAFF NEEDS AND PROVIDE ADEQUATE SUPPORT IN ANY SITUATION.

84.

With hands that trembled with eagerness, I unhooked the chains and drew back the massive bolts.

IT'S *going to be tight*, said Carl. I thought he was saying it would be all right. *But they were hardly paying me!* It could hardly be tighter. George & Tammy were singing about a pawn shop in Chicago. *I love the bit where she throws down the ring & walks out the door,* I said. *Is that a hint?* he said & I said it was. He had to let go. *Isn't it better to admit it? Isn't it a relief? It is not!* He said, *You'll live in squalor!* & rang Justin. Justin was fit to be tied over my *appalling behaviour. Carl is appalled. Everyone is.* What did Carl say? *I'd be ashamed to repeat it. No man could do more for his wife. Covering your knees with a blanket every time ye drove off for Swansea. But he only does that when he has an audience!* Justin said he didn't *know how he'd lift his head in public.* I was scared too & Dora said *Don't lose your bottle,* The Pentonville voices circled my head like flies. I tried to brush them away. *Write it down, write it down, write it down,* they said.

TO HELP AN INMATE TO ESCAPE OR ATTEMPT TO ESCAPE THE MAXIMUM PENALTY IS 5 YEARS IMPRISONMENT.

ACKNOWLEDGEMENTS

Thanks to Lisa McInerney who published the first ten monologues of *Drunken Driving* in Issue 51, Volume 2 of *The Stinging Fly*. I am also grateful to the Royal Literary Fund for their invaluable assistance when writing this book.

Huge thanks to Julia Copus, Denise Riley, Catriona Crowe and Líadáin for their keen eyes and encouragement. And many thanks as always to Michael Schmidt, John McAuliffe, Andrew Latimer, Alan Brenik and Zoe Turner.

Bram Stoker's *Dracula* (1897) is the source for the epigraphs which precede each monologue apart from Monologue 6 — 'I would watch my colonial tongue if I were you.' — which is from Francis Ford Coppola's film *Bram Stoker's Dracula*, (1992).

The Linton Kwesi Johnson poems 'Time Come' (quoted on pages 7, 35 and 78) and 'Inglan is a Bitch' (quoted on page 59) are taken from his *Selected Poems* (Penguin, 2022).